Scrapbooker's Best Friend™

volume one

———— ♥ ————

Compiled by
Melody Ross

Table of Contents

Introduction	3
How to use your new Best Friend™	4
Achievements	5
Babies	6, 7
Birds & Birdhouses	8
Parties	8, 9
Children	10, 11
Christmas	12, 13
Easter	14
Firsts	14
4th of July & U.S.A.	15
Friendship	16–19
Gardening	20, 21
Halloween	22
Home & Family	23–27
Housework	28
Just Because	29, 30
Love & Marriage	31, 32
Pets	33
Recreation & Hobbies	34
Schooldays	35
Snow days	36
Sports	36, 37
Summertime	37
Thanksgiving	38
Vacation	39
Valentines Day	39

Dedication

This book is lovingly dedicated to the selfless souls all over the world who painstakingly create works of heart to preserve memories for generations to come. I have a great love for anything old, especially pictures, and I am thankful that my ancestors felt it important enough to preserve their life's story for people who they would never even live to know, their legacies mean so much to me. I also dedicate the wonderful & unexpectedly wild success of this book to God, to Him I owe everything. Finally, I dedicate this book to my husband, Marq, oh, how I love you . . . and to the never-ending help, support and laughs that I get from Charity, Kallie & Chelsea . . . I owe you guys the world. Keep on cropping!

Melody Ross, Chatterbox

How to enjoy your new
Scrapbooker's Best Friend™

- ♥ Pick a subject from the table of contents that best suits the picture you're going to put the phrase with.

- ♥ Choose just the right phrase to touch your heart or tickle your funny bone.

- ♥ Apply the phrase with pen or marker of your choice—we recommend the ZIG® Memory System® for best results. Or, create your phrase with a computer font.

- ♥ Remember to include names, dates, and special details!

- ♥ Keep your Scrapbooker's Best Friend™ with you everywhere you go!

Copyright ©2001 by EK Success. All rights reserved. Printed in China. Permission is hereby granted with purchase to reproduce the ideas in this book on a limited basis for personal use only. Mechanical reproduction of any part of this book for commercial gain or any reason, in any form, or by any means, in whole or in part is forbidden by law without written permission of EK Success

Achievements

♥ A journey of a thousand miles begins with a single step.

♥ May all of your dreams become reality!

♥ Whether you think you can, or think you can't, you are right.

♥ If you can't always win, at least make the guy ahead of you break the record!

♥ Immortality lies not in the things you leave behind, but in the people your life has touched.

♥ Never give up, never give in.

♥ Slow & steady wins the race.

♥ The will of the human spirit surpasses all weakness.

♥ Throw a fit . . . just don't quit!

♥ Every great and wonderful thing started out as just an idea.

Babies

♥ Nothing's as precious, or brings so much love, as a brand new baby sent from above.

♥ Look what the stork brought!

♥ Look what we found in the cabbage patch!

♥ Look what heaven sent!

♥ A new bundle of joy, is it a girl or a boy?

♥ Welcome little one!

♥ It's a Boy!

♥ It's a Girl!

♥ I've finally arrived!

♥ I made it . . . now where's the food?

♥ Look out world, here we come!

♥ A brand new little baby boy, to fill our lives and hearts with joy!

♥ A sweet new little baby girl, to bring happiness into our world!

♥ Presenting: The newest member of our family!

- ♥ The hands in the cradle rule our world.
- ♥ We've waited so long for this special day, for a child of our own to be sent our way.
- ♥ My heart belongs to daddy.
- ♥ Daddy's little princess.
- ♥ Daddy's girl.
- ♥ Daddy's little buddy.
- ♥ Daddy's new best buddy.
- ♥ Mama's boy.
- ♥ Mom's new shopping partner.
- ♥ There's only one pretty baby in the world, and everybody has it.
- ♥ Never let a baby know you're in a hurry!
- ♥ Laugh and the world laughs with you, cry and you get all wet.
- ♥ Physics lesson: when a mother is submerged in a dirty diaper, the phone rings.
- ♥ A baby's love is the best of all.

Birds & Birdhouses

- ♥ Home "tweet" Home
- ♥ Everybirdie's Welcome
- ♥ Please feed the birdies!
- ♥ When everybirdy helps, everybirdy's happy.
- ♥ Love Nest
- ♥ "Tweet" Hearts
- ♥ "Tweet" Dreams

Birthdays & Parties

- ♥ It's Party Time!
- ♥ Hooray for Birthdays!
- ♥ Hip-Hip-Hooray
- ♥ The great guest of honor!
- ♥ Let's Celebrate!
- ♥ Happy Happy Birthday!
- ♥ Celebration Salutations!

- ♥ Kids make every day a party!
- ♥ Friends make every day a party!
- ♥ What a party animal!
- ♥ One year older and cuter too,
  Happy Birthday to you!
- ♥ Blow the candles, wish away,
  you're the superstar of the day!
- ♥ Yipeeeee!
- ♥ Look at all these presents, I can handle this!
- ♥ Does my mom know how to throw a party
  or what?
- ♥ One year older my little one,
  life for you has just begun!
- ♥ Birthday time again!
- ♥ The baby social event of the year!
- ♥ Son of a gun . . . look who's one!
- ♥ We love you more every year!
- ♥ Friends and family everywhere . . .
  does this baby even care?

Children

♥ Children pull on our apron strings for a while, but on our heartstrings forever.

♥ Train up a child in the way he should go.

♥ Childhood is a journey, not a race.

♥ Parents hold their children's hands for a while, and their hearts forever.

♥ Out of the mouths of babes . . .

♥ A child so small is fun for all!

♥ Children are God's way of telling us that tomorrow will be beautiful.

♥ Children are angels on loan from God.

♥ Children are life's greatest treasures.

♥ No sound is so sweet as the laughter of children.

♥ To teach a child is to touch the future.

♥ I live to see my children smile!

♥ Kids are number one at having fun!

- A big bunch of happiness in such a little body.
- A smile from a child is packaged sunshine and rainbows!
- It takes a village to raise a child.
- I am a child of God.
- I know I'm somebody, cuz God don't make no junk.
- Every child is a different kind of little flower, and all together, they make this world a garden.
- Mom's garden of love . . .
- I'm trying to be like Jesus.
- Mom's sweethearts . . .
- Mom's precious treasures . . .
- These kids were raised on home-grown love!
- Kids are flowers in the garden of life.
- No matter what, no matter where, it's always an adventure if kids are there!
- MONSTERS FOR SALE . . .

Christmas

♥ We believe in Christmas . . .

♥ We love Christmas . . .

♥ Christmas is family near, words of good cheer, memories dear.

♥ All hearts come home for Christmas.

♥ Christmas makes memories.

♥ Family and friends are the true gifts of Christmas.

♥ Country Christmas. . .

♥ Holiday Happiness . . .

♥ Home is the heart of Christmas.

♥ Warm Holiday Fun . . .

♥ Have a holly jolly Christmas!

♥ Christmas glows with love.

♥ Come and see . . . the Christmas tree!

♥ Have a "beary" merry Christmas!

♥ There's no place on earth like a kitchen at Christmas.

- ♥ He's the reason for the season.
- ♥ Follow the star, He knows where you are.
- ♥ Jesus is the heart of Christmas!
- ♥ A season with a precious reason.
- ♥ Wise men still seek him.
- ♥ We believe in Santa Claus!
- ♥ Santa stops here!
- ♥ Santa's Workshop . . .
- ♥ How much longer must we wait?
  . . . please dear Santa, don't be late!
- ♥ Just for Santa . . .
- ♥ Reindeer Crossing . . .
- ♥ Dear Santa, I've been soooo good!
- ♥ Dear Santa, I want one of everything!
- ♥ Are you naughty or nice?
- ♥ He's making a list . . .
- ♥ You'd better not pout!
- ♥ The children's eyes on Christmas night,
  could light the town with sparkling light.

Easter

- ♥ "Hoppy" Easter!
- ♥ Having an "egg"stra special Easter!
- ♥ Some "bunny's" having an Easter egg hunt!
- ♥ It's never too early for chocolate!
- ♥ He is Risen.
- ♥ Spring has sprung!
- ♥ The thrill of the hunt . . .
- ♥ A hunting we will go, a hunting we will go!

Firsts

- ♥ Look who's walking!
- ♥ Your first step towards your journey in life . . .
- ♥ All great journeys begin with the first step.
- ♥ Practice makes perfect!
- ♥ The first time is the hardest.
- ♥ If at first you don't succeed, throw a fit, and then try again.

4th of July & U.S.A.

- ♥ God bless America!
- ♥ We love Liberty!
- ♥ We love America!
- ♥ We love the U.S.A.
- ♥ Sparkling glitter way up high, fireworks light up the sky!
- ♥ America, our country!
- ♥ There's nothing like watching a kid watch a parade!
- ♥ What a grand old flag!
- ♥ The good old U.S.A.
- ♥ The few, the proud, the family of a military man.
- ♥ We want YOU . . . to come home from duty
- ♥ We let dad go away to help the U.S.A.!
- ♥ Red, White, & Blue . . . for me & for you.

Friendship

♥ Friend to Friend . . .

♥ Best Friends . . .

♥ If friends were flowers, I'd pick you!

♥ Friends Forever . . .

♥ Friends are flowers in life's garden.

♥ Meet as strangers, leave as friends.

♥ Good Friends, Good Food . . .

♥ Friendship lives inside your heart,
  Friends together, friends apart.

♥ The seasons may come & go,
  but friends last forever!

♥ The road to a friend's house is never long.

♥ Family & friends are life's gifts!

♥ Good friends are God's way of taking really
  good care of us.

♥ Friendship multiplies our joys & divides our
  sorrows.

- ♥ Nothing is better than time to spend, laughing and talking with you, my friend.
- ♥ Friendship is a gift tied with heartstrings.
- ♥ The best antiques are old friends!
- ♥ Chance made us neighbors, hearts made us friends.
- ♥ Certain things about our friendship never change, like age and weight.
- ♥ Back door friends are always best.
- ♥ Sit long, talk much . . .
- ♥ Stay awhile . . .
- ♥ Friendship warms the heart.
- ♥ A real friend stays when the rest of the world walks out.
- ♥ Real friends listen with the heart.
- ♥ Live well, laugh often, love much.
- ♥ A kind word warms the heart.
- ♥ Friends love at all times.
- ♥ Friendships are tied together with heartstrings.

Friendship, continued . . .

♥ A friend is someone who understands your past, believes in your future, and loves you today just the way you are.

♥ A friend is someone who knows everything about you and loves you anyway.

♥ Life is a patchwork of friends.

♥ Hearts of a feather flock together.

♥ Old times are sweetest, old friends dearest.

♥ The circle of friendship never ends.

♥ I lost my smile, you gave me yours, which helped me find my own again.

♥ Friends become our chosen family.

♥ In my Father's house are many mansions. I hope yours is next to mine.

♥ Plant seeds of friendship.

♥ Friendship often ends in love, but love in friendship never ends.

- ♥ Friends have the art of giving from the heart!
- ♥ There's no gift to compare to a friend who s always there.
- ♥ No treasure is greater than a friend that is true.
- ♥ I am wealthy in my friends.
- ♥ A true friend is a uniting of souls.
- ♥ Your friendship makes a difference!
- ♥ My world is a little nicer because of you.
- ♥ Friends are the sunshine of life!
- ♥ A friend is a gift that keeps on giving.
- ♥ Friendship blossoms in loving hearts.
- ♥ Real friends know your secrets, think not of your weaknesses and strengthen your every footstep with unconditional love.
- ♥ The seasons may come and go, but friends last forever.
- ♥ A friend's smile makes your heart grin.

Gardening

- ♥ Scatter seeds of kindness everywhere you go.
- ♥ Never enough thyme.
- ♥ To plant a garden is to believe in tomorrow.
- ♥ You are my sunshine!
- ♥ Welcome to our garden of love!
- ♥ Spring brings out the gardening in me.
- ♥ May your day be filled with sunflowers & roses!
- ♥ Bloom where you're planted.
- ♥ Plant kindness, harvest love.
- ♥ Gardening tills my soul.
- ♥ You're one in a melon!
- ♥ Gardeners know all the best dirt!
- ♥ Life began in a garden . . .
- ♥ Thyme began in a garden . . .

- Love is the little things blooming forth.
- HOME GROWN!
- Let love bloom!
- Take time to smell the flowers along the way.
- If I had a flower for every time I thought of you, I could walk forever in my garden.
- From one small seed of kindness, love grows.
- Friends are the sunshine of life.
- Plant the seeds, hoe the weeds.
- I love gardening!
- I love my garden!
- You reap what you sow.
- We raise fresh, blue ribbon kids!
- Keeper of the garden . . .
- My life was in a drought, and your friendship was a rainstorm.

Halloween

- ♥ Have a boo-tiful Halloween!
- ♥ Happy Haunting!
- ♥ Best witches!
- ♥ Just say Boo!
- ♥ Will spook for treats . . .
- ♥ Spooky greetings!
- ♥ Too cute to spook!
- ♥ Just a spooky little greeting to wish you happy trick-or-treating!
- ♥ Trick-or-treat, have a sweet!
- ♥ What a feat for just a treat!
- ♥ Halloween kids are such a treat!
- ♥ Please, oh please, let me see what you have dressed-up to be!
- ♥ BOOOOOOOO TO YOOOOOOOO!
- ♥ MONSTERS FOR SALE!
- ♥ Havin' a Happenin' Halloween!

Home & Family

♥ The family circle never ends.

♥ This a home where love dwells.

♥ Home Sweet Home . . .

♥ Home Sweet Country Home . . .

♥ Bless our home . . .

♥ Love lives here . . .

♥ Love at home . . .

♥ We believe in happy hearts.

♥ This house believes in love.

♥ Let's be happy while we're here!

♥ Families are forever . . .

♥ Together is a wonderful place to be.

♥ May love be the heart of this home.

♥ When I count my blessings, I count my family over & over again.

♥ Our family is God's way of taking really good care of us.

Home & Family, continued...

♥ Hugs handed out here!

♥ Love begins at home!

♥ No matter what, no matter where, it's always home if love is there.

♥ This house is established with love.

♥ Fingerprints make a house a home.

♥ Love makes our house a home.

♥ Life's happiest memories are homemade.

♥ Our family is raised on love.

♥ Home is where the heart is.

♥ Home is where you hang your heart.

♥ Loving hearts make a house a home.

♥ Home is where our love grows.

♥ Family is the best kind of friends.

♥ A house is made with nails & beams, a home is made with love & dreams.

♥ Home is where your "HUNNY" is!

- ♥ Mom s precious treasures!
- ♥ Mom's busy, take a number.
- ♥ Mom's sweethearts . . .
- ♥ Time spent mothering is time never lost.
- ♥ A mother's love is forever.
- ♥ Mothers touch the future.
- ♥ Moms make memories . . .
- ♥ We laugh, we cry, we make time fly, such friends are we, my mother and me.
- ♥ There's a quiet place in Heaven for a mother with boys!
- ♥ There's a special bathroom in Heaven for a father of girls!
- ♥ Anyone can be a father, but it takes someone special to be a daddy!
- ♥ Inside of every man is a little boy who wants to come out & play!
- ♥ The greatest gifts I ever had, came from heaven, they're Mom & Dad.

Home & Family, continued...

♥ Sisters listen with their hearts.

♥ Sisters are forever friends.

♥ If sisters were flowers, I'd pick you.

♥ A daughter is a little girl who grows-up to be a friend.

♥ When Mom says no, call 1-800-Grandma!

♥ A Grandmother's love is like no other.

♥ When the going gets tough we go to Grandma's!

♥ There's no place like home, except Grandma's!

♥ Grandparents are flowers in the garden of life.

♥ Grandmas are just antique little girls!

♥ Grandpa is the next best thing to Santa!

♥ We're the apples of our Grandparent s eyes!

- ♥ God could not be everywhere,
  so he created Grandparents.
- ♥ One of the nicest things about marrying
  your son is gaining parents like you.
- ♥ The value of marriage is not that adults
  produce children, but that children produce
  adults.
- ♥ Inside of every man is a little kid who wants
  to come out & play.
- ♥ One is not born a man,
  one becomes a man.
- ♥ Today's mighty oak is yesterday's little acorn
  that held it's ground.
- ♥ Immortality lies not in the things you
  leave behind, but in the people your life
  has touched.
- ♥ A family is a patchwork of personalities tied
  together with heartstrings.
- ♥ This is no ordinary family!

Housework

- ♥ If you've come to see me, come on in, if you've come to see my house, you'd better make an appointment.

- ♥ I clean my house every other day, this is the other day.

- ♥ Housework makes you ugly.

- ♥ I hate 4-letter words: wash, dust, iron, diet.

- ♥ The only self-cleaning thing in this house is the cat.

- ♥ BLESS THIS MESS!

- ♥ Organized people are just too lazy to look for it.

- ♥ Cleaning the house while the kids are still growing is like shoveling snow while it is still snowing.

- ♥ It must be the maids day off!

- ♥ Welcome to Grand Central Station!

Just Because

♥ The smallest good deed is better than the grandest intention.

♥ Let gratitude for the past inspire us with trust for the future.

♥ The smile on your face brings a smile to my heart.

♥ It is easier to ask for forgiveness than to ask for permission.

♥ It's not what we have, but what we enjoy that constitutes our happiness.

♥ Imagination is intelligence having fun.

♥ Blessed are we who can laugh at ourselves for we shall never cease to be amused.

♥ If it weren't for caffeine, I'd probably have no personality at all!

♥ I told you not to stand between me and my chocolate!

Just Because, continued...

♥ If it weren't for the last minute, nothing would ever get done.

♥ Never squat with your spurs on!

♥ Don't bother driving me crazy I know my way on foot.

♥ Some days you're the dog, some days you're the hydrant.

♥ It's never too late to have a happy childhood.

♥ Happiness is meant to be shared.

♥ A smile is a curve that sets things straight.

♥ Happiness is found in the little things.

♥ Let a smile be your umbrella.

♥ One person can make the difference.

♥ Set aside some dreaming time.

♥ When you smile, the whole world lights up.

♥ Simple pleasures are priceless treasures.

Love & Marriage

♥ Happiness is being married to your best friend.

♥ Let's grow old together!

♥ United in love.

♥ Together is a wonderful place to be.

♥ How lucky that we two should meet and make each other's life complete.

♥ A kiss and a hug on this day of love.

♥ Who would have guessed on that first date, that together forever would be our fate?

♥ Nothing is so pure and sweet, as two make each other complete.

♥ I have a friend for a lifetime & more, someone to laugh with, need & adore.

♥ Look what we started!

♥ My life is fulfilled because I share it with you.

Love & Marriage,
continued . . .

♥ The best examples we've ever had,
  was the undying love of Mom & Dad.

♥ To love is to listen.

♥ Friendship often ends in love,
  but love in friendship never ends.

♥ Love is a gift that keeps on giving!

♥ A man chases a woman until she catches him.

♥ Every oak tree started out as a couple of
  nuts who decided to stand their ground.

♥ If at first you don't succeed do it the way
  your wife told you to.

♥ Smile, it's the second best thing you can do
  with your lips.

♥ You and I are like honey & tea,
  I boil & steep . . . then you sweeten me.

♥ Together Forever . . .

Pets & other animals

♥ Pets make a house a home!

♥ Cats make purrrfect friends!

♥ Cats leave paw prints in your heart!

♥ A house is not a home without a cat!

♥ 3 spoiled cats live here!

♥ If you've come to see me, come on in,
   if you've come to see the cat,
   you'd better make an appointment.

♥ Love me, love my dog.

♥ If you want the best seat in the house,
   you'll have to move the dog.

♥ 2 bossy dogs live here.

♥ The dog may invite you in,
   but the kids will scare you away!

♥ WARNING: Attack Goldfish!

♥ We love our pets!

♥ We Love Animals!

Recreation & Hobbies

♥ I fish, therefore I lie.

♥ You catch, you clean.

♥ I golf, therefore I am!

♥ When in doubt, go golfing.

♥ Gone golfing . . .

♥ Crafters are BAZAAR!

♥ When the going gets tough,
the tough get crafting.

♥ She who dies with the most
scrapbook pages done, wins!

♥ Quilting keeps you in stitches.

♥ Quilts warm the heart.

♥ Homemade with love.

♥ There's no fury like a woman
whose kids got into her craft stuff!

♥ There's no fury like a dad
whose kids got into his tools!

School Days

♥ School days, school days,
keep the Golden Rule days.

♥ My first day of school my mommy cried
but I went on a fun bus ride!

♥ My favorite subjects are lunch & recess . . .

♥ I'm no fool, I love school!

♥ My teacher has class!

♥ Going to school is really cool!

♥ I sent my baby to school today,
and knew that he would learn & play,
I sadly wiped my tears away,
he (she) just gets bigger every day.

♥ BACK TO SCHOOL!

♥ GRADUATION CELEBRATION!

♥ The years of school go by so fast,
so I am going to have a blast!

♥ My school is soooooo cool!

Snow Days

- ♥ Let it snow!
- ♥ We love snow!
- ♥ THINK SNOW!
- ♥ Snowmen will melt your heart!
- ♥ Snow days are Mother Nature's gift to us!
- ♥ Happy Winter!
- ♥ Welcome Winter!

Sports

- ♥ Baseball diamonds are a boy's best friend!
- ♥ We're having a "ball."
- ♥ Ballet keeps me on my toes!
- ♥ Ballet is tu-tu much fun!
- ♥ Basketball hot-shot!
- ♥ My "goal" is to play hockey! (or soccer)
- ♥ Best of "PUCK."

Sports, continued . . .

- ♥ Hockey (or soccer) fills my goal!
- ♥ Football (or soccer) is a kick.
- ♥ I'm running for my life!
- ♥ Tennis, what a racquet!
- ♥ Tennis "serves" me right!
- ♥ Volleyball "sets" me in the right direction!
- ♥ I like to spike!
- ♥ I have a drive to dive!
- ♥ Swimming is a "stroke" of genius!

Summertime

- ♥ You are the sunshine of my life!
- ♥ When life gives you lemons, make lemonade!
- ♥ Sizzlin' summertime fun!
- ♥ Ahhhh, the sweetness of summer!

Thanksgiving

- ♥ Give Thanks!
- ♥ Be Ye Thankful!
- ♥ A thankful heart is a happy heart!
- ♥ Have an attitude of gratitude!
- ♥ Let us be thankful unto the Lord!
- ♥ Happy turkey day!

Vacation

- ♥ When the going gets tough, the tough go on vacation!
- ♥ On vacation is the place to be!
- ♥ When in doubt, go on vacation!
- ♥ Relaxation & recreation make the best kind of vacation!
- ♥ Vacation = Relaxation + Recreation
- ♥ FAMILY FUN!

Vacation, continued . . .

- ♥ Wonderful water weekend!
- ♥ The great outdoors!
- ♥ We've "resort"ed to vacationing.
- ♥ Exciting reuniting!
- ♥ Vacations are such a "trip"!

Valentine's Day

- ♥ Happy love day!
- ♥ Be my valentine!
- ♥ Be mine!
- ♥ Kiss me!
- ♥ A kiss & a hug on this day of love!
- ♥ U-R-A-Q-T
- ♥ My heart is full of love for you!
- ♥ There's always time for chocolate & flowers.